Wispers from Heaven

JAKE GRAY

Copyright © 2021 by Jake Gray.

All rights reserved. No part of this publication may be reproduced, distributed, or transmitted in any form or by any means, including photocopying, recording, or other electronic or mechanical methods, without the prior written permission of the copyright owner and the publisher, except in the case of brief quotations embodied in critical reviews and certain other noncommercial uses permitted by copyright law. For permission requests, write to the publisher, addressed "Attention: Permissions Coordinator," at the address below.

ARPress
45 Dan Road Suite 5
Canton MA 02021

Hotline: 1(888) 821-0229
Fax: 1(508) 545-7580

Ordering Information:
Quantity sales. Special discounts are available on quantity purchases by corporations, associations, and others. For details, contact the publisher at the address above.

Printed in the United States of America.

ISBN-13:   Softcover   979-8-89356-277-4
           eBook   979-8-89356-276-7
           Hardcover   979-8-89356-197-5

Library of Congress Control Number: 2024903322

Contents

My Girls 1
If You Ask Me Why I Am Grateful 3
Life, A Gift From God 4
February 2011 7
I Am So Grateful 8
Faith 4/7/11 9
I Think I Am Going to Testify 10
God–Father, God + Man 11
Women Misused and Abused 12
What is Love Based On? 13
Empty Vessel 15
The Impossible Dream 17
The Historian 19
Children of Today–1970 to 2011 20
To My Husband 21
The Rape of the Black Man 22
Beautiful People 23
Your Child My Friend 24
The Reward of Being a Mother 27
Don't Break Your Mothers 30
Jesus and Advi 31
Slide Fox 32
Time 33
Time 34
As I Pass this Way 35

Restaurant 36
From this Day Forth 37
Love 38
The Turn Around Kids.. 39
A Life of a Tree.. 41
Autumn 10/14/11 44
Wind/Love 45

My Girls

They are sunshine on a cloudy day.
When it's cold outside they make
It feels like the month of May, my girls.
I am so blessed to have such wonderful girls.
They make me cry sometimes,
but they make me laugh most of the time.
I am so blessed to have them in my life.
There is *Sherry, Sheena, Arlene Marie, Ernestine Susan.*
When I feel down all I need is to hear from one or all of them.
They cheer me up because they have the *juice*, ha, ha!
I am ever grateful to God for being in my life
and for giving me such a great gift.
My Girls—I Love them so much.

They help make complete make days worth starting,
Planning and loving.
They make you laugh, cry and be proud.
They make you feel like a queen and a king.
Because they are wrapped up with love from above and within.
Because they know in their little minds and hearts they have
Parents who love life and a god up above,
Who loves them and will give life more beautiful.
It hurts you to see how some people dog their life like
Life owes them something.
When this gift was brought with such a great price.
Life doesn't owe is anything, we owe all to life.
Which is Jesus our beginning and should be our end.
God don't make us a prisoner with his love.
He demands us to love him, with all of our
Hearts, Soul and minds.
We can love each other but when man makes these demands,
He is selfish, he can't even see you loving or serving god,
Much less another person on this same earth.
Only him and him alone or nothing or no one,
They will even kill or threaten to have this insane emotion
They call love.

J. CURRY

If You Ask Me Why I Am Grateful

1. To have a loving Father God

2. Jesus our savior.

3. A loving family—Father, Mother, sisters and brothers, etc.

4. A good husband.

5. Good employees that me and my family.

6. Skills to make things happen.

7. Venture some only read about.

8. God beautiful earth, the change of season, the birds, all the creatures big and small.

9. I am most grateful for the love he put in my heart and mind for others and myself.

Tis so sweet to trust in Jesus.

Life, A Gift From God

As I look back on my life and now,
Looking over my present condition,
This is how I found life to be.
I see life as a great gift from God,
Something to be treasured and well lived.
So often we hear this phrase, life rob us,
But that is so untrue it is we who rob life.

All the things that make life worth living
Is ours for the asking.
My father God said,
To ask anything in my name
And it shall be given,
All we have to do is ask.
When I came to realize this
I extend myself out to him,
See because I always believed in God.

I was introduced to him in my early age,
When I was around fourteen,
When I gave myself to Him,
I didn't serve him like I should,
But oh! How the desire was there so deep within,
But being young there was a distraction in between.

But I am glad I found him,
And he accepted me before it was too late.
Getting back to life's gift
If we accept Jesus Christ into our hearts,
We are making a great step already as getting the best out of life.

It is such a great experience to be saved,
Everything is so different,
We have our trial and tribulations,
But to suffer and know Jesus make it so beautiful,
He promised never to leave us.
And that the least we can do to pay for such a great gift
Is to care for one another.

When it became hard to pray think back on the cross.,
And when we think on the word life,
This word should come to mine love.
God so loved the world,
He gave of his only begotten son, that love.
We should be able to give great gifts to God
And others around us.

I have such a love for life that all I can do,
But put myself in its way to be used and to love.
I love god with all my heart and mind,
That he asks of each who pick up the cross.

And then there's a man in my life,
Who helps me make meaning.
He helped bring me back to God,
See he was praying when I wasn't.
He knew about life and about its gift,
And he cares enough to seek this gift for me.

And I love him for being what he is,
Not always what I want but,
Being humble enough,
Be still but the Father who
Molds us all.

Who loves and follow after Him,
This love I speak of bring one.
Things back to my mind,
My favorite poem.

February 2011

Feb. 21st: This is the first day I have set at my desk attempting to write.

Blessings

G is for Blessing only God can give.
O is for faith that we must have to receive your blessing.
D is for gratefulness we must be for all our Blessing.
God so loved the world he gave his only son so we may seek
and request our Blessing.
So, to sum it all up "GOD"

Blessings

I Am So Grateful

When I look back over my life,
I can see plain as day they never think we went through.
But God never left me alone,
As a child I learned that he would never leave us alone.
And you could count on his promise.
I look to Him, and He blessed me.
God taught me you don't have to be rich to live well
You just have to have Him in your heart
And mind and do His *will*.
I love to sing Oh!
Now I Love Jesus *because he first Loved me*.
I was already blessed before I knew Him
Because He knew me first and loved me.

Faith 4/7/11

Oh!! How I Love Jesus because he first loved me,
What a gift one that shouldn't be tossed aside,
Because he is always there for me.
I can't stop talking about Him.,
He is *real*, trust him, tell him your needs and wants,
He knows before you ask but we must be humble and ask.
I Love the Father and the Son, Holy Spirit,
You can't make me doubt Him,
I know too much about Him,
He loved me before I knew him a real Father.
All this, gave me the faith put all things in his hand,
There is a song I love to sing,
I love to sing it's worth, it sounds like music to my ears.
Oh, how I love Jesus,
Thank you God for all your beauty and wonders and love.
Thank you Lord.

J.O.G.

I Think I Am Going to Testify

I first heard about the wonders of God when I was a toddler. My mother would read out of the Bible the birth of Christ. The Christmas story.

Then when I was older, we went to church and one day God sent a godly woman into our neighborhood, and she would have all the kids that wanted to know about God.

And she taught us a song that gets me so excited and goes like this: Oh! How I Love Jesus, and it means so much to me. Why you ask, because he first *Loved Me*. Just like a parent we love our children before we even see them. Just think God so loved the world that he gave only Son to save a sinner like me. And I am so glad that Jesus lifted me and saved my soul. I might live like I should always, but I stopped and listen, so I go back to God with clean hands and a pure heart. Thank you Jesus. God is so good to me I can't stop talking about Him.

God is so real you can't make me doubt Him.

Just waking up is a blessing. And looking at all the wonderments and I know only God never be taking for granted.

I look up and know only *God* He is wonderful I love Him so much. I never said I wouldn't tell anyone about God.

I can't help but tell everyone and anyone who would listen about the goodness and wonders of God, it's all around. Let go and let God. He loves you also give and in return He will give you. Thank you, God, I Love you so very much.

God—Father, God + Man

There is no Greater Father than Father God. If men would take example of our Father God. We would have a lot of good men. Where does it say in the Bible that men had to be hard and strict where there is no reasoning.

God is a *parent*, loving, forgiving, not unreasonable, abusive or uncaring. God takes care of all our needs, he is forgiving, caring, he never leaves us alone. He never makes someone or something more important than His children. I am so glad He first loved me and been around to raise me these 69 years never leaving me alone. Answer my cries, showing me right from wrong. He gave us rules to live by that life can be good. He gave his only son that all the rest of His children can have a better life.

Women Misused and Abused

As a child I grew up seeing men abusing women,
The ones they said they *love*.
Back then I couldn't get away from the crudent.
Seem like every home had this going on.
I thought it was alcohol and arguments.
I had told myself I would never marry a man who drank,
And I would not argue.
But I fell for someone who didn't drink,
A con man, a preacher.
I didn't have to talk back or argue he was just a bully.
I was glad I left before one of my children got killed or myself.
Only good thing that came out of being,
With him was my girls, my joy.

What is Love Based On?

I found love to be based on many misgivings,
I found it to be very one side.
You give and other person just takes without giving anything in return,
It has been like that all my life.
My life is a steppingstone for another,
Person to climb or grow.
And when they reach their goal,
I am just cast aside with a broken heart and emptiness.

There goes my reason for living,
I based my love on hope and dreams,
I based my love on feelings one for another,
The love God speaks of,
"Love ye one another, do not do onto others as we would not
have them to Do us, Trust, Sharing and Understanding."
I find these are for story book children.

Love does not exist it is a thing of the past,
I just came along a little too late.
I am not feeling sorry for me,
I am just stating facts and feeling sorry,
For those who never experience love and loving another.

My love I feel for others makes me a better person.
It makes me happy it makes me worth living.
So often I gave it and the feeling of what
I have received only made me want to die.

Old death was not ready for me,
So, I keep slipping in and out of love.
Unfortunately, love is never returned to me,
It is abused, misused and refused . . .

Empty Vessel

Today as I sit with this pen in my hand with no thoughts or dreams,
I feel like an empty vessel with nothing to give
And receiving the same "nothing."
No special person or thing in mind to make me feel full until,
I overflow with Love and Joy and Peace and Happiness.
I have once known life today to seem so meaningless,
It doesn't even seem worth living.

But I live on to empty to die for,
If I was full of sickness there would be a chance of dying.
But no, I am healthy as can be with no aims or direction to go.
I am not only empty but kind of broken up too,
With no mending power and too weak in mind to look up,
And call on you "Father God" to look down on this vessel.
And mind it and then to fill it until it overflows,
With love and life and all the things that make each day
Worth getting out of bed for.

I look at a pitcher I own it's beautiful,
It's art glass with no flaws and with nothing in it.
It's full funny but you see the person who gave it to me,
is full of love for God and for her fellow man
And life, so I feel it is full.

Here I am, a person who at one time was so full of Love
And Life and for everything around me.
I felt like a beautiful vessel so perfectly put together,
So happy just looking around and looking
Upon my children and my husband and to take care of them,
And love them was everything
I wanted to do each and every day.

But God you played the biggest and best part in my life.
The day I found you were real in my soul.
And then you surround me with so many beautiful people,
Who sang praise in your name,
And played such prayers of faith,
These are things which kept me full each and every day, and now,
I lost all and I don't know how or if I will ever make it back
Where I may be a useful vessel.

I feel if I ever find love again,
For this is what I need so very much,
For when I am in love,
So may other beautiful things happen to me.
Who God? Who! will mend this broken vessel,
Then fill it until it over flows…

The Impossible Dream

I Had a dream of one day possessing,
All the beautiful things that life has to offer.
Starting with me to be beautiful, a dream walking.
Than to be supply with whatever it takes to supply a dream
clothes, Jewelry, car, money and a beautiful home.

A man who can possess my soul my mind, all of me,
Because all he could see was me, a love that would never die.
To shower me with riches of this earth.
To make me laugh when I was in the deepest pit.
To make me cry just to think that one person
Can be so loved by another.

What ear of joy to know it is,
I, who captured his heart and mind
And made him captain of my soul.
In my small mind I hold a Dream someday
He will come along the man I love.

But to now, I hold close in my Impossible Dream,
But you see, I already met the Man many years ago.
He has given so very much of himself even thou it does not show.
He made me rich with treasures the world can never take,
of heaven dream and promises that still exist even when I was awake.

If you look upon me, you will see I am not Beautiful,
I am not rich with the things of the world.
But I have the man who captured my soul,
And he has given much more than money can buy,
He has given love, his kids to share my dream.
We have our love, and we have each other,
it may not seem like much, after all I said I like.

But in the shape, the world is in today we are rich
Because love is hard to find.
In times like these it makes you wonder,
What dreams are built on today no love not even a dream.
I can't help but to want to cry when,
I look at my riches, my jewels and my captain.
Then I realize, It's no longer a dream
but a reality of "My Impossible Dream."

The Historian

I feel like, a historian who has been through the mill
With so many stories,
I can hardly sit still.
About love affairs and broken hearts and disappointments too.
I don't know where to begin or is this because I'm through.
Because these are things which happen in the past
And we all know it's true.

It happened to our ancestors
And it's happening to me and you.
The future is unknown stat that only fate may know.
But this is something no man can ever say is that "I told you so".

For the future is not for us to say,
For all we can do is plan and pray.
Until old fate happens along our way to tell us to stay or go.
I know I may not be famous.
I know I may not be known.
But I know I have made history because
I have a heart of stone.

Wise men say that fools wish in where angels fear to tread.
So, I guess that is why we fine so many dead.
Too many used their hearts instead of using their head.
I have traveled that route, but it left me wounded, can't you see?

Children of Today—1970 to 2011

First God
It is said to *honor* thy mother and father and your day will be long.

They seem to have no time for God or His word.
I guess if he would text them maybe or maybe not.
Sex, text and drugs and game
Give them a game or a phone a whip and a gun.
So, mom and dad know who's Boss.
They show no respect because you owe them,
They didn't ask to be born.
How can they be so wrong?
You love them and protect them,
Then you need to get protection from them.
That is because they don't fear God,
The father, the *father* and the parent of us all.
Trust this the punishment is more severe than they can ever know
And no one to protect them from it trust this.
Honor thy father and mother said Father of us all

God

To My Husband

Thirty years of love the first day I saw your face,
I didn't realize what was taking place.
A union of two lives that multiple into four.
Nothing so incredible has happen to be before.
I loved you than I love you now
And sometimes even more.

I know we had our ups and down.
And sometimes,
It seems like war.
Many battles.
Never keeping score.

Our love has out lasted and open many doors.
Our children was our prize that grew before our eyes.
And time marched on before we realized.
We score a perfect score thirty years and I even love you more.

Happy anniversary

The Rape of the Black Man

Oh! What fools we are to believe we are to illiterate and couldn't be taught or to think intelligently TRICKED into darkness with our eyes wide open. Taking advantage of used and abused, made to work from sun-up until sundown to service others in every way possible with our bodies and our minds and not being able to refuse, raped in every way imaginable, men STRONG Black Men.

We stand in the light of time, and nothing changes we are still being raped and sodomy with no defense, with the justice system turning its head. Why have we given up, lost our faith sunk so low, because no one hears our cry, no one sees the blood spilling into our streets, no one feels our wounds. So, we throw up our legs and open our arms and embrace the rapist trying to ease the pain. The result of these rapes ends also in pain and hurt a lot more than the victim, it hurts his loved ones and all those like him. Because there seems to be no better tomorrow, and the disease keeps spreading.

Oh! What a crime this is. Oh! What a loss. "BLACK MEN, STRONG BLACK MEN RAPED."

July 17, 1996

J. Curry

Beautiful People

The world has a saying, beauty is only skin deep.
But I said it goes farther than that.
The real beauty comes from within a body;
It comes from the soul and the heart.
It is a state of mind, it comes from God,
And he made us beautiful because he made us his own image.
And my God is beautiful, everything he made is good,
he said so himself.

You cannot make me doubt him because today,
I can truly say I know too much about him.
I always consider him a great artist just looking at his
work in nature. But now since I give myself to him,
He shows me, everything is beautiful in its own way.
He gave man this beauty and left him with the decision,
To let it shine, that the world may see it.

I am so glad I yield myself to Father God
And let him guide me to wherever he may.
I love the way he has led me to all the paths and journeys,
For I know no cross, no crown.
I found him to be just what he said,
he would if we let him come into our hearts.
In my daily walk-through life with God,
I meet so many beautiful people . . .

Your Child My Friend

I know you lost your baby not so long ago,
You know you will see her even though
Time goes by so slow.
She has not left you lonely,
A vacation she was in need of.
Thing of this world are sometimes harder than we can bear.
So, God sometimes steps in
And He takes us From this earthly home
to heaven for some Rest,
because He knows our work on earth
Will take us to our death.
We know how she was a blessing
to all the lives she touched
Even though she was just a baby
She gave the world so much.

It's a crime what's on your mind,
So, stop listening to your heart
And what you're thinking
Because it's real!
You will go to Jail with no bail it's all real.
You do the crime you do the time.
Big brother is watching you>>just a reminder!
Work not for Jerks so became a clerk and stay alert!
Don't get caught up in something you thought up
Because it's wrong, you must be strong.
If you want to save and buy a ride, get a job.
Don't steal keep it real or you will go to jail.
So, stop listen to your heart and what you're thinking.
Don't get caught up or the noise you hear
Will be cell doors clinging.

Jeanette curry

Oh! How I love thee I cannot begin to count the ways.
There are some little girls in my love life to
and they range From age 6 thru 11.

The Reward of Being a Mother

I myself, am the mother of four lovely daughters. They were a joy to me from the very beginning of their lives. I had so much pleasure watching them grow into little people, learning to "make sounds and smile," seeing the changes rolling over, sitting up and holding on trying to walk. I began saying to myself "Here comes the real fun, catch me if you."

And oh boy! trying to understand what they were saying was another test. I wouldn't have wanted to miss any of it for truly it was special. Son, they could *talk* and *walk*, then *run* and *drive*.

Then difficult changes began, and I felt maybe I should not have children was I doing a good job as a parent. We mothers doubt ourselves. All we can do is pray and ask *God* for *guidance*. With all these changes we make it through, and the rewards are great. The children become wonderful adults, good friends and good citizens.

The rewards of being a mother: I myself am a mother of four lovely daughters. There was a joy to me from the very begin of their lives. I had so, much pleasure watching them grow into little people, learning to make sounds and smile. Seeing the changes. Rolling over, sitting up and holding on trying to walk. I begin saying to myself "here comes the real fun catch me if you can" and oh boy! Trying to understand what they were saying was another test. I wouldn't have wanted to miss any of it for it was truly special. Soon they could talk and walk, then run and drive. Then difficult changes began, and I felt maybe I should not had children, was I doing a good job as a parent? We mother doubt ourselves. All we can do is pray and ask God for guidance with all these changes we make it through the rewards are great. The children become wonderful adults. Good friends and good citizens. And with luck and god blessings we become grandparents to my girls: Sherry, Sheena, Arlene and Susan—love.

MOM

Subj: PRINCE KEYON
Date: 6/11/2010
To: *nicolekeyon2171@msn.com*

My name is Keyon. Say that? Not Leon, Keyon with A.K. I just arrived today. I am my daddy baby and he so proud. He waited so patient just for me. And here i am born to be free for the world to see just little me. When I look in my mom eyes I can see love me. And I was meant to be a little boy with a great heart and lots of love for thee. If you met my dad, you already know me. Because he's a man I like to be. I would like to thank god for us three. Me and my whole family.

Love grandma jeanette

Friday, June 11, 2010, AOL: Jeanette O. gray

Don't Break Your Mothers

From the time of birth on this earth she loved you.

She was so proud to say out loud this is my son, he's a good one, he's a strong one and a smart one. With love in her heart a smile on her face something only you can replace with sadness and sorrow and disgrace. I told you show you right from wrong. I lead you I feel you. I taught you, I brought you. Why did you go wrong? Did you not love me all along? Was I wrong, was I not strong? You were such a beautiful baby the boy of my dreams. The smile on my face you erased. My heart full of joy you empty it into pain . . . Was I so blind or were you so vain. You broke it my heart and I gave you such a good start.

                    Jeanette curry   7/23/2004

Jesus and Advi

The day I met Advi,
I knew she was a gift Tiny as she was.
She gave the world a great, big gift.
We as parents love her and her great big kiss.
The talent that she has,
It is something that can't be missed
Jesus loves her, yes, I know
Because the bible tells us so.
Advi can sing, draw and dance.
I believe that she can bless us all,
Oh, how I love Jesus because,
He first loves me/ her/ us all.

Slide Fox

Once upon a time, there were three hot chicks, Red Riding hood, Goldilocks, and Cinderella. One day, they were all talking about a cute guy. But they didn't know his name, so they went to the place where they heard he hang, at the farm.

So, off the three went looking for the farm where he hung out.

They all walked in and there he was, swagging over to Little Miss Muffet.

And they walked until he was close to her, and they rush him saying, "Don't believe a word he's saying because he is a fox. A Slide Fox who can't be trusted."

And he turned around and couldn't believe his eyes; all of the women he tried to fool. But this time, he knew his Goose was cooked.

Amen

62nd Birthday

Time

There are times in our lives,
We should all be told,
How special we are.
And how much we are loved.
Jake, time has come to the kindest,
Hardest working man
I have ever known.
Jake, my children and
I want to say *thank-you*,
For your love and kindness.
So, tonight is your night.
We want to give
You back some of
The happiness
You have given us.

Time

Time passes so slowly as if it is unconcerned.
The minutes, seconds and hours oh,
How my heart burns but it's when
I'm with you that it feels like good wine.
The kind we would devour in just a little time.
The times we spent together were so precious and so sweet.
It makes time so unbarring until the next that we shall meet.
If I was to possess the power to halt the hands of time.
I'd put in my pocket and have all behind.
The minutes and the hours would be what it would be a
servant to my Feeling and the things that divine me.
I don't possess the powers to halt the hands of time.
For I'm just another stranger passing in the night
And being overcome by time.
It is just a losing fight,
For time would be the winner for that
The way it's planned to leave it in the hands of God,
Not in the hands of man.

As I Pass this Way

As the 21st century close I am still alone. Waiting for love to find a home. A home in my heart and my life. I never thought I love so long and be so alone with no magic. No laughter no warmth. I suffer in silence with a broken heart. If ever I should pass in this cold indifferent world, I certainly wouldn't last as long. For you, see this old heart of mine is made of glass. It's been bump and dump step on broken totally in half.

Restaurant

7/20/2008 Sunday

The restaurant

Last night I went to a restaurant called music. The chefs were serving food for the soul. It was wonderful and filling, it fills the mind, the heart, and the soul. The food was served in Jesus name. The main meal was the dixie humming birds. So, refreshing the flavor was a hit with everyone they loved it. The price was right all you had to pay was an open heart and mine in Jesus name. They served an old recipe one that was good for my dear mother and those who believed or was raised on such food. A meal like this is enjoyed all around the world and refused by none. This food is good to every race of people all around the world that old time religion good stuff praise god.

From this Day Forth

From this day forth,
I will tell the world that
I will take you as my wife,
I will do this for life.

I will give you my all,
And always stand tall,
Because you are the love of my life.

From this day forth,
I am your man,
Count on me,
You always can.
Your husband,
your biggest fan.

I love you today and this day forth.

Love

Love is so illosuse it faster than the wind. You're in and out before it begins. I tried to hold it tight in my hand because when I put in my heart that when it runs. Then I come to realize I am not the only one searching for this illusion one the one we call the wind/but the one we know as love.

Address 1   Address 2   Address 3   Phone Email

The Turn Around Kids

4/22/12

I have 2 daughters that were headed in the wrong direction and God step in and gave them another go at life. The drugs were stop and just when they weren't sure of what was next, he gave them a purpose in life that is so wonderful and rewarding. I am so proud and happy that their way was not the end, but God's way was their beginning *praise* God.

So, the lesson learned is, you too can become a turn around kid also. Just look up and ask God and he will lead you to the right way.

Jesus keeps us near the cross, there is one for each of us.

Sherry, Sheena, Arlene & Susan Years apart 58

61-62-64

All that was going on back then, shape them in the wrong direction. But raised in the church they were soon realized what God had in store for them. Life back then was hard enough but to keep up was only going to get harder. So, seeing what can be next was to ask God to lead them. And so, they went to church sometimes and listen to the word and decided to change their route.

That rode they start was going to be long and hard.

So, the turnaround kids got on the right path led by God, and today life is so much better.

Praise God, thank You, Jesus.

They are now the turnaround kids.

A Life of a Tree

Once in a huge forest, stood a small seedling, very low down near the ground, and over him stood these very big trees; shading him with their very large umbrella-like tops... Keeping out the beautiful sunlight and the mist which moistened their lovely tops.

This little seedling became very depressed because it didn't seem to be growing, and it often stood in its place in a droop-like position... like it had no will to live. But one day, in depression, it decided to seek help, and it would raise its weak, small limbs to the other trees around it and asked, "What must I do to live?" Being so small and the trees around it so large, they didn't hear its cry for help.

So again, he became discouraged, and dropped its limbs to its side. But wait... there was a friend to all little seedlings, someone who was probably responsible for it being in the very place where it stood. Someone so wise and so strong, who has the power to reach the lowest and the highest places anywhere around, and this friend was the Mighty Wind.

One day, when the forest was very still and quiet, the Wind blew down from above to speak to this little, troubled seedling... to advise him what he must do in order to grow. The Mighty Wind said, "First, you must drink enough water to strengthen your limbs, then you must raise your limbs in order to pray".

The little seedling was eager to obey, but did not understand what he had heard, and thought the Wise Wind had said to play. The little seedling did not know too much about playing either, because first of all, he did not have any friends near him that were his size. So, he tried to talk to the birds, and the smaller animals and ask them to play with him, but they scurried about, ignoring him. He even sought the friendship of the small insects, that sometimes walked upon his tender body, but no one wanted to play with him.

So again, depression set in and this time, he almost died!

Then, one day, the Mighty Wind decided to look in on his little friend, to see how he was doing And when he did, he was very upset, "Oh, dear", said the Wind. "What's the matter with you?" Didn't you follow my instructions that I gave you?" The little seedling replied, "Oh yes! I tried to find someone to play with me, but no one would play with me, and I drank the water and it made my limbs strong, but then they got tired of standing up, and no one paying any attention to me . . . so here I am . . . "Oh, my poor, little friend," said the Wind, "you misunderstood me, I told you to pray, not to play; you will have plenty of time to play when you reach the top, but first you must reach this point in your life. Okay?"

"Now, listen very closely to what I am saying", said the Wind, "First, take a large drink of water to strengthen your limbs, now raise them up toward the other trees, for there you will find more strength and each day you will find yourself growing a little taller. Then you will soon receive some new food for strength . . . this is called the sunlight, and with this your body will take on a new look . . . it will grow round and green; you will be a real beauty. But you must never look down again. You must keep looking up and praying, for there is strength in prayer.

And beyond the tops of these trees, you will witness something more beautiful than you have ever seen. A beautiful blue sky, and in this sky, you will, in the daytime see the sun from which you receive your very much need strength, and also, beautiful clouds which some days turn dark to give you that much needed water to strengthen your limbs and give your umbrella its beautiful color.

And at night, you will witness something more beautiful than you can ever imagine . . . and this is the heavens in all its glory, a clear blue sky with jewel-like forms which seem to dance, and these are called stars. And there is an added attraction, which is called the moon, which, if you look closely, it seems to be smiling at you. All this that you see when you reach the top, is the welcome committee; welcoming you to a brand-new life; one which will mystify you, but you will love every bit of it.

And above all these heavens, there is a God, the Ruler over us all, and the One who made you what you are. So, every day, raise your leaf-laden arms in prayer. And then you can play in the breezes that I blow softly among the trees. Good-bye, my friend," said the Mighty Wind.

"Good-bye, Mighty Wind, and thank you very much", said the happy seedling.

Jeanette Curry April 20, 11974

Autumn 10/14/11

God if I should die before I wake,
Please let it be in Autumn.
My favorite time of the year,
To go in such splendor my soul would happily surrender.
My life on this earth was blessing.
I learned a lot, I loved a lot and even laugh a lot.
Because my *father* God gave me a lot.
A lot of love and wonderful people in my life,
Who taught me a lot.
I am happy for my parents, sisters, brothers, nieces and nephews.
A great man in my late years.
Most of all four wonderful children and grands.
And added member to my life young men,
That are like sons to me.
I love the sunrise, the sunset,
The rolling clouds and blue sky.
The color of the trees and rustling from the wind.
My favorite time of year *Autumn*.
This isn't a goodbye,
But a sweet surrender.
Thank You father God, I Love You

Wind/Love

Two four letter words = both destructions,
And sometimes kind
It's amazing how these two compares,
not only in its Destruction but also in its fear
It tears you up and twist you around
and leave you Lying on the ground.
Breaking up and turn around
Blowing in and out our lives
Two four letter words that's destructive
and Sometimes kind; both can be the same
They can put a smile on you or make you your mind.

Printed in the USA
CPSIA information can be obtained
at www.ICGtesting.com
LVHW011725210524
780584LV00003B/8

9 798893 561975